Contents

Foreword

Volleyball was founded in 1895, and is now a major sport in over 170 countries of the world. It is popular both as an informal recreative game which can be played anywhere and by anyone, and as an international sport with a strict code of rules. It is an ideal game for playing in schools and on beaches, and as a sport in its own right it is of the highest worth – demanding speed, agility and stamina. Above all, it is great fun, and its requirements with regard to space and equipment are modest.

Know the Game Volleyball is based on the rules compiled by the English Volleyball Association, which in turn are derived from those of the International Volleyball Federation. It was the first book about volleyball to be published in Britain, and it has been regularly updated.

I hope that this most recent edition will give new readers as much pleasure and information as it has to the thousands who have already bought a copy.

Don Anthony
President, English Volleyball Association

Note Throughout the book players are referred to individually as 'he'. This should, of course, be taken to mean 'he or she' where appropriate.

Cuba and East Germany are two of ▶ the many countries in which volleyball is played

Introduction

In 1895 William Morgan, the Physical Director at Holyoake Y.M.C.A. Gymnasium, invented a game in which an inflated bladder was 'batted' by two teams over a rope. Morgan wanted a simple sport which would be suitable for a variety of physical types, both fit and unfit, and which could be played almost anywhere. This one served the purpose, and was dubbed 'volleyball'.

The game spread throughout the U.S.A. and elsewhere. In 1947 the International Volleyball Federation was formed; in 1953 volleyball was introduced into the Pan American Games; and it became an Olympic sport at Tokyo in 1964. It is now the top-ranking recreational team game in the world.

Volleyball has been an Olympic sport ▶
since 1964

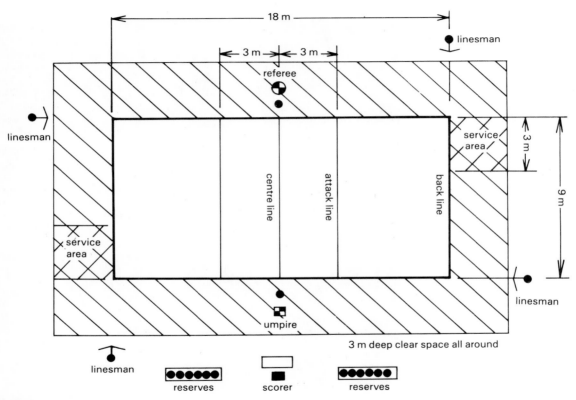

Fig.1 The volleyball court

The court

Fig.1 shows the court as specified by the International Volleyball Federation. The playing surface is 18 m (59 ft) long by 9 m (29½ ft) wide, including the outer edge of the lines. These lines are 5 cm (2 in) wide, and should be at least 2 m (6½ ft) from all walls or obstructions.

A line 5 cm (2 in) wide is drawn across the centre of the playing surface separating the two courts. In each court an 'attack line' is drawn across it, 3 m (10 ft) from and parallel to the centre line.

Two lines 15 cm (6 in) by 5 cm (2 in) and 3 m (10 ft) apart are drawn at the back of the end line to permit service from anywhere between them and the end line. The service area is a minimum of 2 m (6½ ft) in depth.

The surface of the playing area may be ash, earth, grass, wood or a composition surface.

The net

The net is 1 m (3 ft) deep and 9.5 m (31 ft) long. It is made of 10 cm (4 in) square black mesh, and a double thickness of white canvas or linen, 5 cm (2 in) wide, is stitched across the top. A flexible cable passes inside the band of canvas, and stretches the upper edge of the net; it is essential that the net be taut, for the ball may often rebound from it and still remain playable.

Two tapes made of white material, 1 m (3 ft) long and 5 cm (2 in) wide, are fastened near each side of the net, perpendicular to the side lines and the centre line.

Coinciding with the outside edges of

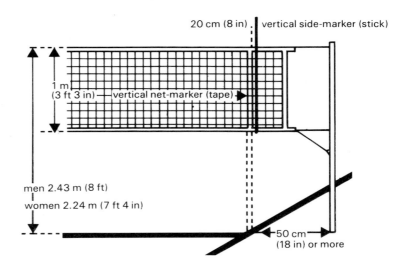

Fig.2 The net ▶

the tapes, two flexible antennae are fastened to the net at a distance of 9 m (29½ ft) from each other. They are 1.8 m (6 ft) long, with a diameter of 10 mm (⅓ in), and should extend 80 cm (31½ in) above the top of the net. They are made of fibre-glass or similar material, and should be of contrasting colours, alternating in 10 cm (4 in) long sections.

The side markers and the antennae are considered to be part of the net.

The net is supported at each end by a pole; it must be the same height from the ground at each end, and not more than 2 cm (⅔ in) above regulation height. The regulation height of the net at the centre is 2.43 m (8 ft) for men and 2.24 m (7⅓ ft) for women. The height for juniors and children is left to the discretion of national associations.

Equipment

The ball

The ball is spherical, with a circumference of 65–67 cm (26 in) and a weight of 260–280 g (9–10 oz). It is made with a supple, laceless leather case, inside which is a rubber bladder.

Players' clothing

Members of the team must appear on the court dressed alike. The players each wear a shirt or vest, shorts, and rubber or leather shoes (without a heel). It is forbidden to wear headgear or any other article, e.g. a bracelet or watch, which can cause injury to other players.

All players wear numbers: 15 cm (6 in) high on their backs and 10 cm (4 in) high on their chests.

Start of play

There are six players in each team, regardless of the circumstances. A team with less than six players automatically forfeits the game.

Choice of court

The two captains toss a coin to decide which team will serve first: the winner chooses either the right to serve first or the court in which he wishes to start the match.

After each set, the teams change courts and the team which received service to start the set serves first in the following one.

Before the beginning of the decisive set, the referee tosses the coin once more to fix the choice of court or service.

In the last set, when one team has a total of eight points, the teams change courts automatically; however, the team serving at the time of the change continues to serve.

Position of players

At the time the ball is served, the players of each team must be placed in their own court in two lines of three; these lines may be broken ones.

The players nearest the net (nos. 2, 3 and 4) are the front line players; the other three (nos. 1, 6 and 5) form the back line. The numbers refer to the positions and not the players in them, so during the course of a match a player will play in all six positions.

As soon as the ball is served, each player may cover any section of his own court. The same player serves until his team loses a point, and both teams stay in their original playing positions. When the serve passes to the other team, this team rotates clockwise by one position before serving.

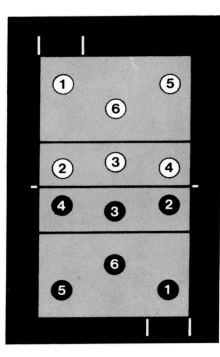

Fig. 3 Position of players ▶

The rotation order must be observed until the end of the set. Before the beginning of each set, this rotation order may be changed, on condition that the change is denoted on the score sheet.

Players of the back line

The rules prevent back line players from doing two things:
1. They may not play the ball directly from within the attack area into the opponents' court unless the ball is below the height of the net.
2. They may not block.

From their own area, back line players can return the ball by any means permitted. A back player smashing from his own area may land on or beyond the attack line ('spiking line'), providing his take-off for the smash is clearly behind the attack line.

If the back line player is outside the court but in the extension of the attack area, he is considered to be in this area.

7

The service

The service is the means of putting the ball into play. The player in position no. 1 stands in the service area and strikes the ball, having tossed it into the air, with one hand (open or closed) or any part of the arm. The server is not allowed to strike a ball resting on the other hand.

The server must stand behind the end line and between the lines limiting the service area. Having served, he may enter the field of play.

If the ball falls to the ground without being touched by the server, the service is retaken, but the referee must not allow the game to be deliberately delayed in this fashion.

The service is considered correct if the ball passes:

a over the net without touching it into the opponents' court, and
b between the two vertical antennae marking the width of the court.

The service is a foul if the ball:

a touches the net
b passes over or outside the side antennae above the net
c touches a player or object before going into the opponents' court
d goes under the net
e falls outside the limits of the court.

If the serve is faulty, the referee indicates 'side out' and the opponents gain service.

The game in action

Play is started by a service from the player in position no. 1. The team receiving the service attempts to return the ball to the serving team's side of the net, using three hits or less (with the exception of contacts when blocking). No more than three hits are allowed, nor may any player hit the ball twice in succession.

If the team receiving serve loses the rally as outlined on page 18, the serving team scores a point. If the serving team loses the rally, no point is scored (except in the deciding set), but the receiving team gains serve. Except in the deciding set (see page 18), only the serving team can score points.

◀ The service, using an open hand

8

Handling the ball

The ball may be played with any part of the body above the belt. A player who touches the ball or is touched by it when the ball is in play is considered to have played the ball.

The ball can touch any number of the parts of the body down to the belt, on condition that this is simultaneous, that the ball is not held but hit, and that it rebounds vigorously. If a player touches the ball more than once with any part of his body, before any other player touches it in the meantime, he has committed a foul (a 'double hit').

The best way of playing the ball accurately is with a volley pass. The ball must be clearly hit; if it comes to rest momentarily on the hands or on the arms of the player, this is considered to be catching or holding. Scooping, lifting or shoving the ball is also considered to be holding.

The volley pass ▶

Simultaneous contact

If two opponents simultaneously hit the ball above the net (see fig.4), the player from the team on whose side the ball does *not* fall is deemed to have hit it last. The other team then has three touches of the ball.

If, after the simultaneous touch, the ball falls on the ground *inside* the limits of the court, the team on whose side the ball falls is at fault. If the ball falls *outside* the court, the other team loses the point.

If two players of the same team play the ball and touch it together, this is considered as two touches (except in the case of a block). If only one player contacts the ball, it is considered to be one touch.

If two opponents make a personal foul simultaneously (a 'double foul'), the point is replayed.

Net play

If the ball touches the net during play (other than the service) and passes into the opponents' court, it is not a fault. Even if the ball goes into the net, it can

◀ Fig.4 Simultaneous contact

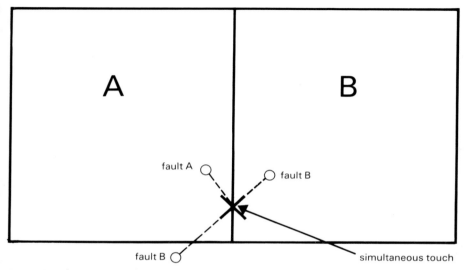

Fig. 5 Simultaneous touch

still be played by any player other than the last one to touch it, providing that the maximum of three touches is not exceeded. If the force of the ball hitting the net causes the net to come into contact with an opposing player, this does not constitute a fault on the part of the latter.

If any player touches the net, he commits a fault. If two players from opposing teams simultaneously touch the net, this is known as a 'double fault', and the point is replayed.

This player must be careful not to ▶ touch the net

Crossing the vertical plane of the net

It is a fault to hit the ball from within the playing space of the opposing team, or to cross the vertical plane of the net with any part of the body with the purpose of interfering with or distracting an opponent while the ball is in play.

It is *not* a fault to pass the hands over the net (with or without touching the ball) when executing the block or when the hands are inert, nor to cross the vertical plane of the net without touching an opponent or the opponents' court.

Passing the centre line

It is a fault for any part of a player's body to contact the opponents' court during play.

It is *not* a fault for a player to touch the opponents' court with his foot or feet, provided that some part of the foot or feet remains in contact with the centre line; nor is it a fault to enter the opponents' court after the referee has whistled to stop play.

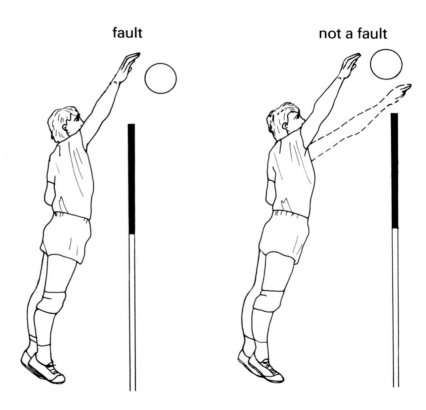

fault   not a fault

Fig.6 Crossing the vertical plane of the net ▶

Blocking

Blocking is the action at the net of attempting to intercept a ball coming from the opponents' side. A player is considered to have the intention to block if he is in a position at the net, and places any part of his body, from the waist upwards, above the height of the net.

Blocking can be performed by any or all players in the front line. Any *attempt* to block is considered to be an *actual* block only if the ball is contacted by one or more blockers.

A team which has effected an actual block has the right to three more contacts before returning the ball to the opponents' area.

Any player participating in a block in which the ball is contacted has the right to make a successive contact. However, such a contact counts as the first of the three hits allowed to the team.

Substitution

Each team is allowed a maximum of six substitutions per set. All substitutes and coaches must be at the side of the court, opposite the referee, either sitting on the team bench or in the designated warming-up area.

Substitutions may only be made when the ball is dead, e.g. during a time-out, between points, etc. Each team is allowed two time-outs per set (see this page). If the substitution is not completed immediately, a time-out is awarded against the relevant team. If this team has already exhausted the allowable number of time-outs, it is penalised by loss of service or loss of a point.

During the pause for a substitution, the coach is allowed to advise the players. All players entering or leaving the court must have the permission of the referee and must report to the scorer.

Any player beginning the set may, in that set, be replaced only once by a substitute. He may permanently re-enter the set only in the rotational position he previously occupied. A substitute leaving the game may not re-enter it in the same set.

If a team becomes incomplete through injury to any player and if all other substitutes have been used, a substitute can replace the injured player even if he has already played in another position.

Time-out

A 'time-out' is a half-minute pause for rest or substitution, or both. A captain or coach can appeal to the referee or umpire for a time-out when the ball is dead, but each team is allowed only two time-outs per set.

If a time-out is utilised for major tactical talks, the coach must address the players from outside the court, near the team bench.

Time-out for obvious injury is three minutes. If the referee notes an accident, the game is stopped and the point is played again.

The referee controls the players and other officials

Officials and discipline

In competition class play the following officials are required: first referee, second referee, scorer and four linesmen. In simple, recreational games, one referee and a scorer will be adequate.

The first referee

All decisions of the referee are final, and he has absolute authority over the game and all other officials.

The referee uses a whistle to signify the beginning and end of games, a point, change of service, foul, etc. In top class play a referee's platform is also essential, similar to that used in lawn tennis, only higher.

The referee warns any player who:
a disputes with the referee or an opponent
b shouts on court, with the intention of distracting or intimidating the officials or opposition
c intentionally delays the game in any way.

He gives a personal warning to players who repeat the offence. A personal warning is recorded by the scorer and penalised by loss of point or service. After two warnings, or for any particularly unpleasant behaviour, the offending player is disqualified, but he may be replaced by a substitute.

The second referee

The second referee places himself on the opposite side of the court to the first referee, and assists him in every way.

The second referee notes the players' positions at the start of the game, authorises substitution, and keeps a check on all 'time-outs'. He draws the first referee's attention to unsporting play, and blows his whistle for faults concerning:
a crossing of the centre line
b crossing of the line of attack ('spiking line')
c contacts with the net.

The scorer

The scorer positions himself opposite the referee, and takes note of the score. He also notes all 'time-outs', substitutions and any other interruptions.

Before the set begins the scorer takes the names of the players, substitutes, captains and coaches. He receives from the captains or coaches the positions of the players on court, and ensures that the rotation order is kept during the match.

The referee on the right is standing on a raised platform

The linesmen

If four linesmen are available, they are placed at the four corners of the court. If only two are available, they are placed at diagonal corners, away from the service areas.

The linesmen are under the orders of the referee, who can amend their decisions. They raise their flags when the ball is out, and point it down when the ball is in court.

Duties of players

Every player must know the rules and keep strictly to them. During the game a player can only address the referee through the captain of his team.

The following offences by players, substitutes and coaches are punished:

a persistently addressing the officials about their decisions

b making unpleasant remarks to officials

c committing unpleasant acts or actions tending to influence the officials' decisions

d making personal remarks to or acting unpleasantly towards opponents

e deliberate coaching during the game from anyone outside the courts other than the coach (except during time-out).

Sanctions are as follows:

a for a slight fault: a single warning

b for a serious fault: a personal warning recorded on the score sheet, which automatically entails the loss of a point or exchange of service (whichever is applicable). If the offence is repeated, the referee may disqualify the player for the set or match.

Management and leadership

Managers, coaches and captains have team discipline as their responsibility.

The coach cannot interfere with the referee's decisions.

The coach may request 'time-out' (see page 13) and 'substitution' (see page 13). When the game is interrupted for a time-out, the coach has the right to speak to players, but may not enter the court.

The captain is the direct manager of the team on court, and the only member of the team who may address the officials. If the team has no manager or coach, the captain assumes all duties.

◀ Note the second referee who is closely observing play

Scoring

Points

The serving team scores a point when:

a the ball touches the ground inside the opponents' court

b the opponents have played the ball more than three times consecutively

c an opponent holds or pushes the ball

d the ball touches an opponent under the belt

e an opponent touches the ball two consecutive times

f an opponent touches the net

g an opponent reaches over the net to play the ball, except to block or hinder a player of the serving team

h an opponent reaches under the net and touches the ball or any opposing player when the ball is in play on that side

i an opponent completely crosses the centre line

j at the moment of service, the opposing team commits a fault of position, e.g. after winning service has not rotated clockwise

k a returned ball crosses or touches the net outside the antennae which determine the width of the court

l a returned ball goes out of court, passes under the net, touches an object outside the court, or is returned by a player aiding himself with any object as support

m an opposing back line player in the attack area incorrectly returns the ball (see page 7)

n an opponent receives a personal warning

o the opponents delay the game in a persistent manner

p the opponents illegally replace a player

q the opponents prolong the interruption of the game for more than half a minute (see page 13).

In every set except the deciding one, only the serving team can score points. If the non-serving team wins a rally, it gains the right to serve rather than a point.

In the deciding set, if the serving team wins a rally it scores a point and continues to serve; if the receiving team wins the rally, it gains the right to serve and scores a point.

The set

A set is won by the team that first scores 15 points, with a minimum lead of two points. If the score reaches 14–14, play is continued until a two point lead is reached (e.g. 16–14 or 17–15). However, a point limit is reached at 17, i.e. if the score is 16–16, the team scoring the next point wins the set with only a one point lead.

A match is won by the team that gains three sets, i.e. each match is the best of five sets.

Fig.7 The scoresheet ▶

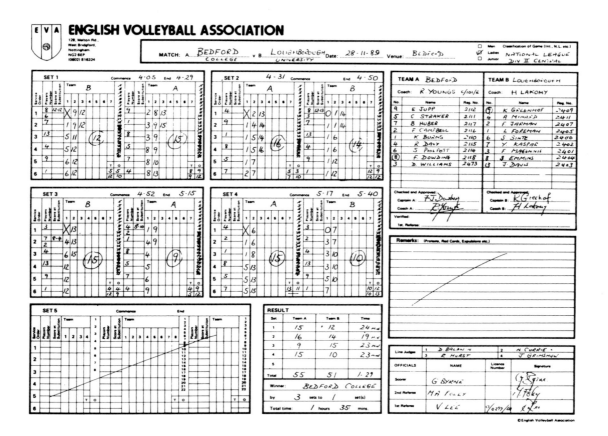

Skills

The serve

Play is initiated by the serve, and it is an essential skill for playing the game. There are three accepted methods of service: the underhand serve is the simplest and should be used by beginners, but the overhand tennis and 'windmill' serves are more potent in high class play.

Spin can be added to all three methods by striking across and through the ball when serving.

The movement when serving is a rhythmic one in which the whole body plays a part, not just the arm and hand alone. The knees are bent and then stretched, and the arm follows through after contact with the ball.

The server must always move into his position on the court after serving.

◀ Fig.8 The underhand serve

Fig.9 The tennis serve ▶

Fig.10 The windmill serve

Drills for the serve

1. The players are divided into two groups and line up along each back line: each player serves back and forth to a partner.
2. A target is placed on the court (e.g. a towel or hoop), and the serve is aimed at this target.
3. The court is divided into various areas, with points for each area that is hit with the serve. Fig.11 shows the usual scoring system.

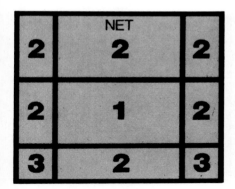

Fig.11 The scoring system for a service drill

The tennis serve

Service-receive

As a team is preparing to attack when receiving service, it is important that the reception of the service be made effectively. Since the majority of balls fall in the area illustrated in fig.12, it is essential to space out the team's players to cover the most vulnerable area.

The most popular line-up at basic levels of play is called the 'W formation' (see fig.13).

Player no. 3 is the setter: all the other players aim to dig the ball to him, so that he can set either no. 2 or no. 4 to smash the ball. In this line-up each player must face his setter and stand in a position where he can see the server clearly.

Nos. 4, 6 and 2 are responsible for balls falling close to the net, at the side of the court and in front of them. Nos. 5 and 1 are 'sweepers' and play all balls falling deep. No. 1 must cover every dig played by no. 6, as this is the most vulnerable area.

All players must call for every ball they play on serve-receive, to avoid confusion.

Fig.12 The court's vulnerable area

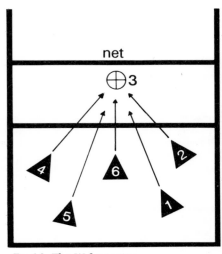

Fig.13 The W formation

The volley

The volley is the two-handed overhead contact used to keep the ball in play, to set up for an attack or to pass the ball over the net.

The ball is played with the fingers and thumbs, which are spread to provide a cup into which the ball will fit (see fig.14). The ball should be contacted above and just in front of (about 6–8 cm or 2–3 in away from) the forehead. For this reason it may be necessary to move quickly into position so that the ball can be played from that point.

The force required to move the ball comes from the legs, arms and wrists.

Fig.14 The volley ▶

The player brings his hands to ear level, with the fingers outstretched; he bends at the knees and hips; he contacts the ball in front of his forehead; the fingers are fully extended as the ball is released, and the legs are straightened

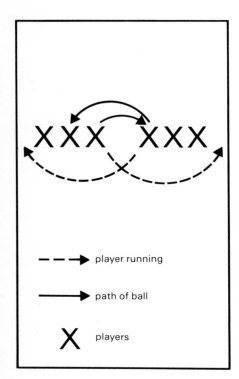

Fig.15 A group drill for the volley

Drills for the volley

One ball per player
1. The ball is volleyed overhead repetitively.
2. The height of the ball is altered: high and low.
3. Volley overhead; volley forwards 2–3 steps; move under the ball; volley overhead; volley back. Repeat.
4. Standing 60–90 cm (24–36 in) from a wall, the player volleys against it, changing the rhythm. The drill is then repeated at a distance of 3 m (10 ft) from the wall.

One ball, two players
1. The ball is volleyed back and forth, varying the distance between the partners.
2. The drill is as above, with a deep knee bend and a jump (or any other calisthenic movement) between the volleys.
3. The first player volleys the ball and then jumps, sits, bends or makes another movement; the second player must mirror this movement when he has volleyed the ball.

Group drills
1. The players are in two lines facing each other, and the ball is passed back and forth. After a player passes the ball, he goes to the back of the other group (see fig.15).
2. As above, but the ball is volleyed over the net.
3. Two players (X1 and X2) each have a ball. X1 volleys the ball to X3, who returns it with a volley. X3 moves to a marker in front of X2, who volleys to that position. X2 volleys it back, and returns to the original position. The drill is repeated 20–30 times.

The dig

The dig, or two-handed underhand pass, is used to receive serve (in most cases) and to play a ball that is too low or too fast to be volleyed.

The ball is contacted with the inside or fleshy portion of the forearms. The arms are kept together by the player joining his hands and bending the wrists down towards the floor. The arms are not swung at the ball.

Since in most cases the dig is used to absorb energy rather than to generate it, very little movement is required. Any force needed is produced by the legs.

Drills for the dig

One ball, two players
1. One player tosses the ball to his partner, who digs it back. They change round after 10–15 repetitions.
2. As above, but the partner must come forwards to play the ball. He then moves back to his original position, and the drill is repeated.

One ball per player
1. The player digs the ball repeatedly overhead, keeping the ball in control.
2. As above, but the height is altered: high and low.

Fig.16 The dig ▶

The smash (or spike)

The smash is the chief offensive weapon in volleyball, and consists of hitting the ball downwards, at great speed, towards the opponents' court. It is one of the most difficult skills in the game, but is the most satisfying from the point of view of both the player and spectator.

The setter puts the ball in the air about 3 m (10 ft) above and 30 cm to 60 cm (12–24 in) from the net; a second player takes two or three quick steps in towards the net, jumps in the air and hits the ball at its highest reach point above the top of the net.

To attain maximum height and still remain under control, the smasher should jump off two feet. The approach footwork is illustrated in fig.17. This approach usually requires a player to start about 3 m (10 ft) from the net, or at the attack line.

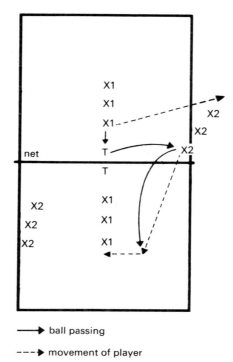

ball passing

movement of player

◀ Fig.17 The smash

Fig.18 A group drill for the smash

Drills for the smash

Hitting a stationary ball
The coach stands on a chair or table and holds the ball close to the net and above it. (The net may be lowered below regulation height for training.) The player uses the approach steps, takes off and hits the ball out of the coach's hand down into the opposite court.

Hitting a tossed ball
1. One ball, one player: once a player acquires the ability to hit a held ball, the coach tosses the ball in the air while standing close to the net. The ball should go at least 3 m (10 ft) above the top of the net.
2. Group drill (see fig.18): a player passes the ball to one of the feeders, and then joins the line-up to smash. After smashing, the player goes round the post, retrieves a ball and joins the line on the other side of the net. For the drill to work, players must continuously run to retrieve the balls.

The block

Blocking is the defensive counter move to the smash. In order to block, the player jumps into the air and stretches his arms out above him. The block can be played by all players in the forward line, but it is usually played by just two.

If the ball touches one or more players taking part in a block, only one touch is counted. Any player who has blocked may then play the ball as a second touch.

Blockers may pass their hands over the net to meet any ball on the opponents' side of the net which is being attacked, even if it is not the third hit.

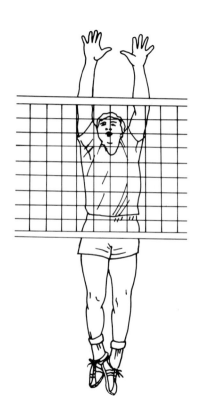

Fig.19 The block ▶

Drills for blocking

One ball, two players

1. The net should be lowered to make it easy for players to reach over it with a slight jump. The two players stand on opposite sides of the net. The first player tosses the ball at a point just above the net and in front of his partner. The partner jumps, puts his hands over the net and pushes the ball towards the floor. The drill is repeated ten times, and the players then change around.

2. The drill is practised as above, with the following variation: the player with the ball jumps in the air to smash, tossing the ball with his non-smashing hand. The other player jumps to block.

3. A blocking drill is incorporated with one of the smashing drills.

Covering

Covering involves moving near a player who is smashing or blocking, in order to play any balls which may rebound or be deflected off the opponents' block and fall near him. This is effected by using the 'W formation' on service-receive.

Covering the smash

After setting, no. 3 follows the ball and moves in close to the smasher to pick up any balls which rebound from the block. No. 6 also performs this function, but stands behind the smasher. No. 2 moves to play any balls deflected sideways from the block. Nos. 1 and 5 cover the rest of the court between them.

All players must stand alert at the moment the ball is hit. Anyone standing 'bold upright' will be unable to move quickly to retrieve the ball.

Covering the block

Using the same formation as above, no. 6 stands just behind the 3 m (10 ft) line on service-receive to cover his team's block when the opponents are smashing.

During a rally, no. 6 stands near the 3 m (10 ft) line to cover any balls which rebound there, and moves in to cover a block exactly as described above for the smash. He crouches behind the blocking player to play any balls which touch this blocker and fall near him, or any balls tactically placed over or around the blocker.

The front line player who does not block must remember to drop back behind the 3 m (10 ft) line to cover any balls which rebound there.

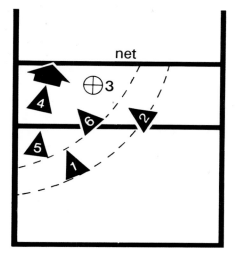

Fig.20 Covering the smash

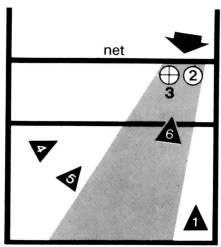

Fig.21 Covering the block

Modified games

There is no reason why volleyball cannot be modified to meet the desires and abilities of those involved. Due to limitations in facilities, physical abilities of players and stages of skill development, it is quite often necessary to adapt the standard international game.

Listed below are some variations that have been used successfully in many parts of the world:

1. Raise or lower the height of the net.
2. Reduce the players in a team to three, two or even one ('minivolley').
3. Reduce the size of the court.
4. Reduce the size of the ball: official volleyballs in a variety of sizes are now available. Correct technique for younger players with small hands can best be developed by using a smaller ball.
5. Play outdoors on grass or a sandy beach.

Volleyball is fun to play on the beach ▶

Glossary of terms

Dead ball After a point, side out or other decisions temporarily suspending the game.

Double contact Ball touching a player twice or rolling along a part of his body.

Double foul Players on opposing sides fouling simultaneously.

Four hits Team hitting ball more than three times.

Good Ball striking ground in court.

Hand over Reaching over net.

Line Crossing centre line.

Net Player touching net when ball is in play.

Net service Serve touching net.

Out Ball touching ground outside court.

Out of bounds Serve passing outside net markers.

Point Scoring.

Side out Change of service.

Time-out Allowable pause for rest or substitution.

Under net Crossing under net contrary to rules.